Espresso Evenings

Espresso Evenings

POEMS BY

EDWARD M. GEORGE

NEWSOUTH BOOKS
Montgomery

NewSouth Books
105 S. Court St.
Montgomery, AL 36104

ISBN 978-1-60306-327-7 (paperback)
ISBN 978-1-58838-080-7 (2002 printing)

Design by Randall Williams
Printed in the United States of America

THIS BOOK IS DEDICATED TO POETS
HELEN NORRIS, HELEN BLACKSHEAR,
AND THE LATE ANNE GEORGE
FOR THEIR ENCOURAGEMENT AND TOLERANCE
OF MY MEAGER ATTEMPTS TO ENGAGE IN THEIR ART.

When power leads man toward arrogance,
poetry reminds him of his limitations.
When power narrows the area of man's concern,
poetry reminds him of the richness and diversity of existence.
When power corrupts,
poetry cleanses.

— JOHN F. KENNEDY

CONTENTS

OBSERVATIONS / 89

MEMORIES

The life of men is a dubious experiment.

— C. G. JUNG

Espresso Evenings

I saw the best minds of my generation destroyed by mad-
ness, starving
hysterical naked,
dragging themselves through the negro streets at dawn
looking for
an angry fix . . .
— FROM *Howl* BY ALLEN GINSBERG

The Village was ripe then
with the spirit
of the Subterraneans.

She was a strange girl
who called herself Starlight
whose ways bewitched
my Southern innocence.

She took me to dark places
in ancient cellars
where there were bongo beats
and espresso machines
and the fragrance of cannabis sativa.
Where black clad hipsters
would nod off in the floor
as the H kicked in.

Where pale young bearded men
would parade out
one by one,
each more morose than the last,

To sit on a tall stool
and drone heavy blank verse
into the morning hours
about things philosophical.

Where sometimes one of the icons,
Ginsberg or Kerouac or Cassady,
would drop by
and bless the masses
with his presence
and maybe find
a lover for the night.

Where I
would sip espresso
in the candlelight
and sit transfixed
by the rhythms of the night
and the Zen-ness of the moment.
By the irony of a restless generation
of brilliant minds
searching vagrant alleys
for their souls.

Neon Haiku

The glow of the city
lights up the sky
hiding the stars.

Chalk Dust

School days, school days
Dear old golden rule days . . .

A few days before they tore down
my old elementary school
I took one last walk
    through the heavy double doors
    and down the oiled oak floors.

My footsteps echoed
    off the high plaster walls of the hall
    where in my mind
    I heard again first graders
    reciting the pledge of allegiance
    and the Lord's Prayer
    amidst the smell of chalk dust
    and white paste.

Then I remembered
    how the bell would ring
    and there would be a clamor
    of hungry youngsters
    headed for the lunch room

where they would drink milk
from little paper cartons
and eat
from thick plastic plates.

And then I walked out back
    into the tiny playground
    where we would play kickball and red rover
    and let out all the whoops and yells
    that we'd held in all morning long.

And there still stood
    the white oak with the tire swing
    where Mary Lou had kissed me
    with precocious lips
    that tasted like Juicy Fruit.

It was hard to bear
    that they would soon tear down
    this monument to memories
    of innocent minds
    opening up
    to words and places
    where they'd never been before

Just so that trickster Progress
    can build a big box
    of glass and steel
    which when its course has run
    will be mourned
    by nobody.

After the Game

On a hard pine bench
in a cold locker room
I sit
after the game.

My head throbbing like crazy.
Left ankle sprained again.
Bruises turning purple on my thighs.
Ribs hurt every time I breathe.

Drops of hot sweat
making little puffs of steam
on the cold concrete floor.

Looking forward
to next week's game.

The Time Machine

Everybody finds somebody someplace.
There's no telling where love may appear.
— DEAN MARTIN

Last week I bought
a time machine.
A black fifty-seven Pontiac hardtop
just like the one I use to race
at the Clanton drag strip.

And as I drive along the streets
of my childhood
I pass by houses long torn down
replaced by parking lots
and print shops
and such.

And talk with friends
not seen in years
some of whom have passed away
or long ago disappeared.

We ride with the windows down
and play the radio
on our favorite station
where the deejay used to let us visit

and would dedicate love songs
to our girl friends.

Right now I ride with Helen
under my right arm
and we talk about the train wreck
that took her teenage life
and how things might have been.

She gives me a squeeze
when the deejay says her name
and dedicates
Everybody Loves Somebody
by Dean Martin.

Yesterday I rode with Randy
and Coy
over to Robert's house
and we all laughed about
how old I'd gotten
in the years since they'd been gone.

I told them that they took
the easy way out
leaving before
everything broke down.

I told Robert that we'd found out
after the accident
that his girl friend was pregnant.
He was forlorn.
He had not known.

He said that means he also lost a son
or maybe a daughter.

But he felt better
after we decided the baby
was in a better place.

Then we listened to
Chuck Willis
sing *What Am I Living For*
and smoked Pall Malls

And rode in silence
past the graveyard
where we had taken a new guy
snipe hunting
and wound up getting arrested
by the police
when they saw the new guy
running down the street
dragging a bag behind him.

And I wondered
what in the world
happened to that guy.

It was just getting dark
when Helen said
that I should take her home
and go back where I belong.

When I kissed her sweet mouth good-bye
and felt her young breasts
against my heart
The pain
was the dark, hollow kind
that digs into your core.

And I knew
as I said good-bye
with tears in my voice
that there are places
that I best not visit
too often
lest I forget to come back.

Childhood Hero

There he was.
        Right in front of me.

It was like coming upon
a starlet
on a downtown sidewalk.
        You don't know whether
        to gawk
        or smile
        or turn away
        and pretend
        you didn't notice.

But there he was.
        Right in front of me
        in the Sears men's room.

My childhood hero
        Ashby Steele
        who could run like the wind
        and once scored four touchdowns
        in a state championship game.

Who was so handsome
        that he modeled
        in commercials
        on local TV

And rode in holiday parades
        with cheerleaders
        and homecoming queens.

Who took the microphone
        in the auditorium
        to lead us in prayer
        when Kennedy was shot.

But who had disappeared
        for years
        and was said to be
        a spy
        or making movies
        in Europe.

But there he was.
        Right in front of me

And I
        not knowing what to say
        almost panicked
        and ran away.

Instead I mutely
    froze in place
    staring blankly
    in his direction

Until finally
    he smiled
    and asked if I
    would move a little
    so that he could
    mop where I was standing.

The Blizzard

Evening had fallen
on Mississippi's flat belly
but we could still see for miles
as the moonlight lay calmly
across the vast whiteness.

The snow was falling slowly
and ironically
upon cotton fields
Softly blotting out
all signs of a road
except the telephone poles
that served as our guides
as Bill and I trudged along
with our load of brightly wrapped
and ribboned Christmas boxes
so incongruous to our plight.

We were hitchhiking
from Montgomery to Memphis
and were halfway there
when the blizzard hit
as we sat drinking coffee
in a country cafe.

With only Bill's army uniform
my windbreaker
and our teenage insolence
between us and eternity
we trudged our surreal route
between the endless sagging telephone wires
through a foot of snow
in ten degree air.

In our moonlit path
new flakes were dancing
with the undulating wind.
Seeing no lights,
no rising smoke,
We both knew
but neither said
that any stop
however short
would be our last.

At one point
Bill broke the somber mood
by holding up a Santa-papered box
and saying
that if things became too much to bear
we could always fade away
in a Wild Turkey haze.

As the miles blurred
one into the other
we would here and there notice
a white tail deer
staggering in confusion
looking wild-eyed
for something familiar.

Somewhere in the middle of
our frigid desert
we came upon an abandoned store
and had decided to break it
into firewood
when a black Chevy convertible
came sliding to a stop
beside us.

A lone sailor
on Christmas leave
was bound for Arkansas
from Pensacola
and could take us to the Helena Bridge
if his car would only stay on the road.

We sifted through the snow for bricks
and concrete blocks
and filled his trunk until
the Chevy sat like a mother hen
its tail feathers scraping the snow.

The sailor said
he had not seen another car
except for one
sitting face-first
in a frozen creek
about twenty miles back.

We stretched out
and half-dozed
in the warmth of the Chevy
until just before the Helena Bridge
he stopped to let us out
on Highway 61
the blues highway
and wished us luck.

We waved
as we watched the Chevy's
heavy-laden rear end
leaving a deep rut
in the snow
that had begun to freeze
upon the road.

Then we once again
took up our loads
and fell into our cadence.
For miles up 61
we walked in silence
through the still amassing snow.
Each of us lost
in his own illusions.

Our thoughts
contorted by fatigue
and the sameness
of a landscape
still wavering
between darkness and dawn
were beginning to run together
like words on
a wet newspaper.

Then just
as the sun rose over
a barn roof
sway-backed
under the weight
of drifting snow
We heard the jingling
of a bread truck's snow chains
and Bill dropped his gifts
and jumped in front of the van
waving wildly
giving the driver no choice
but to stop
or run him down.

The bread truck let us out
at a truck stop in Tunica
where we sat
still shivering
surrounded by stranded truckers
and damp Christmas boxes
drinking heavy cups

of long haul coffee
trying to feel our feet again
hoping there was no frostbite.

Twenty-four hours
and much coffee later
we caught a ride to Memphis
with a Korean War vet
who had correctly guessed
that the snow would then be melting.

When we finally set foot
on a sidewalk in South Memphis
we had been two days
in the same wet clothes
and shoes
and only by habit
were we still upright.

Three days later
hitching back
to Alabama
in the Mississippi sunshine
was like
a magic carpet ride
until this drunk fairy
in a Fairlane
almost killed us
when he passed out
and ran off the road.

His forehead bruised
he let Bill drive
the rest of the way
as he slept it off.
But he kept trying to sleep
on Bill's shoulder
and Bill kept pushing him off.

When I awoke
at the sound of a car door opening
my cheek was pressed hard
against a seam
in the plastic seat protector
but I recognized the shape
of the tree limb hanging above us.
We were in my driveway.
We were finally home.

But as with all adventures
We kinda hated to see it end.

Little Joe's Cafe

Down at the end of Monroe Street
you'd see a five-gallon jar of pickled pigs feet
at Little Joe's place where black folks ate
where lunch was served on a heavy blue plate.

Formica tables with silver legs
a saucer in the middle full of deviled eggs.
Oil cloth checkered in white and red.
Red beans and rice and hot cornbread

Or fatback bacon and a mess of greens.
Red plastic tumbler full of sweet ice tea.
Jukebox in the corner playing the blues.
Old men drinking coffee and swapping news.

A storefront building with a red front door
concrete walls and a concrete floor.
It's all gone now, but we all know
no one pickled pig feet like Little Joe.

The Ice Man

On the top step
to our front porch
I sit
studying the dust
on the toe of my shoe.

I hear the clip clop
of the horse-drawn
ice wagon
on the gravel street
and feel a pang
of impending loss.

Next week
the street
will be asphalt.

And the ice route
gets shorter
all the time.

Little Brother

When I was eight years old
my mother brought home
a brand new baby boy
who stole my heart
and changed my life.

I couldn't wait each day
for school to end
so I could run home
to stand by the railed crib
and watch him reach for me
with stubby fingers
that I would gently cup
in my palm
until he fell asleep.

I loved his baby powder smell
and little baby sounds.
We burped and glubbed together
and somehow I knew
exactly what he meant.

And in his keen blue eyes
I saw a sparkle
when I whispered
big brother secrets
between the wooden slats.

And as he slept
I'd watch
the yellow teddy bear drummer
rise and fall upon his chest.

But one day
when I was in the front yard
being Lash Larue
snapping guns from bad guys' hands
with my dime store whip

I heard my parents burst
through the front door
with baby brother
all wrapped up in a fuzzy blanket.

Without a word to me
they were in the car and gone.

It was the first time
I had ever seen them cry.

It was the last time
I ever saw
my little brother.

Ocean Haiku

The mooncapped waves
caress the shore.
Seagulls rest on the wind.

Just Sittin Around

It was summer 1967
and I was just sittin around
not doin a whole lot
      you know
and all of a sudden
it came to me
that I was just sittin around
not doin a whole lot.

I thought
I ain't got no right
to just sit around here
doin nothin
when there's people in a war
fightin
while I'm just sittin around here
doin nothin.

I ought
to get up
and do somethin to help
somethin I can be proud of.

Lessee
What can I do?
I know.

I'll join the army
and fight in the war.

I might even be a hero
with lots of medals
name in the paper
on tv.

Sergeant,
Gimmee those papers.
Where do I sign?

Well
That was
Nine hundred eight lousy meals
Fifty guard duties
Twenty KP's
Two good buddies
Twenty-five inspections
Fifteen thousand miles
A couple a hundred congs
           trying to blow my head off

At least a million cuss words
Six Saigon whores
Two whuppins
One Dear John
Twelve blisters
One jungle rot
and two dozen dumb bastard sergeants
ago

When I was just sittin around
not doin a whole lot
just listening to
a goddam fool.

Labor Day Trip

We were four GI's
in a sixty-one Ford
heading for Cape Cod
on Labor Day weekend.

A trunk full of booze
and beer and ice.
At every rest stop
we stopped to celebrate.

After eight stops
we'd lost all sense
of where we were going
or why we were going there.

After dark
we stopped for mixers
in Troy, New York
and Dan backed the Ford into the
radiator of an antique Packard showcar

And spilled my purple passion
all over the back seat
and the front
of my white dress shirt.
My chin was dripping purple drops.

Then I was bouncing
all over the seat
as Dan shifted from first
        to reverse
        to first
        to reverse
        to first
trying to pull away with the parking brake on.

And Frank and Tom
were jumping up and down on the bumpers
trying to unlock them
too drunk to notice that
they weren't even touching.

And then a Troy Police car drove up
and the cops calmly watched
the Ford straining to pull away
and Frank and Tom doing their bumper dance.

With me on the sidewalk
in my purple and white shirt
directing this insane ballet
with my empty plastic tumbler.

And then a wild-eyed guy named Tony
came running from the diner
waving his arms
and cursing in Italian
about what we'd done to his Packard.

and the cops finally got out of the squad car
and took names
and asked if we'd been drinking.
We of course said
     no-o-o-o.

They said okay
we'll let you go
     but only if you head
     straight out of town
     and not stop anywhere
     or smash any more cars.

At the first rest stop
outside of town
we stopped
to celebrate our luck
and try to figure out which way to go.

Back on the road we went
for four more hours
and eight more rest stops
but still no closer to the Cape.

At three a.m.
bone-weary and mind-numb
we looked for a motel
to respite our trip
until the next day.

Seeing a sign saying
     Shady Rest Inn

we stopped and staggered
into the lobby
to check in.

The desk clerk did all he could
to tell us why
we really needed
to find another place to stay.

But when we
in our desperate drunkenness
threatened his life
he checked us into room 24 on the mezzanine.

The next morning's sun
awoke a crumpled, stale quartet
      spread out
      on chairs and beds
      and blankets on the floor.

Hoping to find a coffee shop
to dull our throbbing heads
we staggered down the stairs.

From halfway down the stairs
we saw the lobby
crowded with
at least three dozen wide-eyed white-hairs
each at least eighty years old.

Feeling completely out of place
we paid the desk clerk for a day's stay

and reeled on out the front door
to try to find our car.

As we stood around the open trunk
drinking the last of the warm beers
and holding our thumping heads
we read the sign that said:

Welcome to
the Shady Rest Inn
Retirement and Convalescent Home
Peaceful Living Every Day.

A Southern Boy in Boston

Listen to him talk
she told her friends,
pointing at me and saying
Say something
I want them to hear how you talk.

My first impulse was not to talk
but to pound her
on top of her yankee head.

But then I looked at all her smiling friends
some of whom were quite striking
for yankee gals
and thought there might be sex
somewhere in this deal.

There was.

And from then on
I was downright loquacious.

The Lone Ranger

Willie was my friend
when we were nine.
He was cool.
He painted his broomstick horse silver
and declared he was the Lone Ranger.
I painted mine black
and was Lash LaRue.

Then one day
his seamstress mother
married a rich guy from Birmingham
who renamed Willie *William*
and took him away,
saying he needed to stay away
from poor white trash like me.

Many years later
came a call from Italy
and Willie
said he'd be back home
for the step dad's funeral
and would like to visit
his white trash friend.

As we drove through
the old neighborhood

Willie, now *Will*, not *William*,
told me how he'd studied art
in Venice
and disappointed the old man
who disowned him.
But Will said
it was all for the best.

He'd scraped by for years
on looks and charm
but was now a big star
in spaghetti westerns
who could have bought and sold
the step dad.

He said he once got to play
the Lone Ranger
and ride a big silver horse.
I laughed at the thought
of a black Lone Ranger.
Will said okay
it was a pretty silly movie
with a fat Italian Tonto.

But he sure loved
riding that big silver horse
and being
the Lone Ranger.

MUSINGS

One cannot help but be in awe
when he contemplates the mysteries
of eternity, of life,
of the marvelous structure of reality . . .

— ALBERT EINSTEIN

The Messenger

I am the voice
of my generation.
I am the messenger
from my time.

Bicycle Ride

Life
is a bicycle ride.
Sometimes you can coast
but mostly
you've got to peddle like hell.

Rock of Ages

Rock of Ages, cleft for me.
Let me hide myself in Thee.

Desolate
I find myself alone
in a whitewashed country church
    with black hymnbooks
    in racks in back
    of wooden pews
        worn slick
        from fresh pressed
        Sunday-go-to-meeting pants
        and stiff-starched
        cotton skirts.

The site
    of solemn rites
from baptisms
to weddings
to that final ride
by six good men
after the preacher's eulogy
of a you
    who never was
    but maybe could have been.

The smell
        of oiled pine floors
        baked by years
        of morning sun
                streaming through a
                stained glass Jesus
                whose robe
                is now a faded pink.

In the corner
        a worn organ
        that for more Sundays
        than I have lived
        has led the flock in
        Rock of Ages
        and called to
        the preacher's waiting arms
                those whose hearts
                are heavy laden.

This afternoon
I sit alone
in a back pew
where I finally find
peace
in the face
of He
        Whose eyes
        follow me
        Whose hands
        reach out to me

From an old painting
that has hung
    between the windows
    for as long
    as I can remember.

Grandpa's Guitar

Amazing grace
How sweet the sound
that saved a wretch like me.

When I was a boy
it didn't look like
anything special
to me.
Just an old Silvertone 6-string acoustic
probably mail-ordered from
a Sears Roebuck catalog.

The finish worn through
where Grandpa's flannel shirt
had rubbed against the front.

The back a little warped
from being caught in
a rain storm
that hit
the Fourth of July barbeque.

A little crack in the neck
from when Grandpa whacked
a drunk upside the head.

But as I grew older
I learned that
    Grandpa had sat in
    with Hank Williams
when he played
the Bullock County Barn Dance
    one Saturday night.

And he'd
loaned the Silvertone
    to Mother Maybelle
one day
    when her guitar stripped
    a tuning key.

And Grandpa
on occasion
would get liquored up
and go down to
Willie Brown's shot house
and play the blues.
    Rumor is
    he once backed up
    Elmore James.

And once Grandpa
played rhythm
on a record made
during the Depression
that wound up
    in the Smithsonian.

But every Sunday
he'd clean up
his hungover self
and play gospel
at the Mt. Olive
Baptist Church.

The old timers tell me that
he played
Amazing Grace
like an angel.

I own the Silvertone now
and I've used it every place
from Proud Larry's in Oxford
to the Berklee School of Music
where I did a lecture
on hill country blues.

But my favorite times
with the old guitar
are when I sit under
the big oak tree
on the home place
and play *Amazing Grace*
for just
      Grandpa and me.

Miss Liberty

Give me your tired, your poor,
Your huddled masses yearning to breathe free,
The wretched refuse of your teeming shore.
Send these, the homeless, tempest-tost, to me.
I lift my lamp beside the golden door.

— EMMA LAZARUS

Flying into New York
from Boston
I see Miss Liberty
      piercing
      the early morning fog
      with her torch
      of freedom

And
      as the sun gleams
      off her copper face
I have this
eerie feeling
of familial
deja vu
as I think of how
my great-grandfather

and great-grandmother
would have felt
seventy years before

When
as teenagers
they had sailed
on separate ships
into New York
from the old country
not speaking or reading English

And met on Ellis Island
where their family names
were Americanized, sterilized.
But they didn't care
because they had seen
Miss Liberty
and everything would be just fine.

They had relatives
in Ohio
and Alabama
and they would soon be
Americans
and drive big cars
and wave as they passed by
with their heads tilted back
and hair blowing in the wind

Laughing
big American laughs

and smoking
American cigarettes
and drinking
American whiskey
from silver flasks.

What adventure
they must have felt
lay before them.
And wonderment
the likes of which
I'll never have the chance
to know.

And I wish
that they were here now
so that I could say
how much I finally understand
of what they had tried to tell me
all those years ago.

Death of the Twins

Freedom itself was attacked today
by a faceless coward.

— GEORGE W. BUSH

It's been two days now.
But we still can't believe
they're gone.

They'd been the city's pride
Standing bold.
Piercing the clouds
with their magnificence,
their America-ness.

The day they died
the morning sun had gleamed
against their jeweled sides
reflecting in the eyes of
those who teemed the streets below.

But now they lay
in shameful piles.
Shattered pieces
indistinguishable
one upon the other

As brave souls
poke among their entrails
hoping to see
  or hear
  or feel
a sign
of life
But finding none.

Where once the skyline
had starred the twins
there is now instead
A tower of gray dust
and smoke
hovering
covering everything
with death.
Permeated
with the acrid scent
of burnt wire

And the smell
of body parts
waiting
to be collected
in orange plastic bags
and tagged and stacked
in anonymity
while loved ones
pray at home.

On this day
the setting sun
paints the dust and smoke
shades of purple and red and gold
while searchers strive
to set portable lights
so that they might search into the night.

The concrete grit
collecting in the sweat
on their grim faces
goes unwiped
as they strain to place the poles
out of the way of
sliding girders.

All night tonight
and for days on end
this rhapsody,
this dance of desperation,
will continue

Until one day
the body bags will all be full.
The dust all gone,
the air as clear
as city air can be,

And there will be only
our memories
and maybe
a marker

Where once had stood the twins
so tall and proud
gleaming
in the morning sun
opening their glass doors
to those whose days
would celebrate America.

Young Love

It's two a.m.
and drizzling rain.
I'm driving all alone
down some
      long
      wide
      straight
      flat
      ain't nothin happnin
highway
When on the radio
comes Julio Iglesias
singing
"To All the Girls I've Loved Before."

And I remember what
love was like
when I was young.
When love was not a matter
of just your heart
but of every drop of blood
that was in your heart
And every breath
you breathed.
And every synapse
of every nerve.

When you didn't just miss a girl
You ached for her.
You hurt when she was gone.
You filled your thoughts with her.
You tried to imagine what she was doing
at just that second
And you fell in love with her
all over again
and couldn't wait
to tell her
how much you loved her.

And when you did tell her
once again
how much you loved her
how pale the words
compared to how
you really felt.

When you were incomplete
empty
unfeeling
except with her.
When the very thought
of losing her
would shoot through your soul
like a hot rivet
and make suicide
seem simple.

When the world seemed

to disappear
when you were alone with her.
And making love
was like riding a roller coaster naked
through the stars.

When hearing a certain song
or seeing a leaf on the wind
or smelling new-mown grass
would stop your heart
As you thought of when
you heard that song
        or saw a falling leaf
        or rolled in new-mown grass
with her.

And as I drive on
through the night rain
I remember that other dreary day
when she told me it was over
And her words
seemed to rip the skin from my flesh.

And then
with her in my mind's eye
I sing along with Julio:
To all the girls who shared my life
who now are someone else's wife
I'm glad they came along
I dedicate this song
to all the girls I've loved before. . .

The Girl from Mississippi

The first time I saw her
she was fourteen
and so cute
it made my heart hurt.
> But I was twenty
> and it just couldn't be.

The next time I saw her
she was eighteen
and so beautiful
it made my heart cry.
> But I was married
> and it just couldn't be.

The next time I saw her
I was twenty-eight and single
and she was so lovely
it made my heart ache.
> But she was married
> and there was just no way.

The last time I saw her
she was more beautiful than ever.

She'd been prepared so well
you couldn't tell
that she had been pinned for hours
in a twisted metal tomb
in a drainage ditch
off an icy country road.

And now my heart cries
every night.

Love Is Like That

No drink shall ever taste so sweet
as the wine we share tonight.
Nor light ever adorn beauty
as my humble candle worships yours.
Nor kiss ever be so pure
as the kiss that brought us love.

No heart could ever pound as mine
when I hold you in my thoughts.
Nor time ever stretch so endlessly
as when I ache for you.
Nor distance ever be so far
as when you are away,
or even when you're near.

You realize, of course, I'm exaggerating
but love is like that, you know.

Such Beautiful Love

I feel your hand
float cross my chest
to nudge me near enough
to kiss your pulsing temple.
     Your hair tickles the tip of my nose.

I sneeze.
You laugh.
I love your laugh.

We explore
each other
once again
each touch familiar
but new.

Tenderness drifts into passion
    pure passion
       love's passion

That takes us to that magic place
    where there's
       moonlight
         and music

and the air
      smells likes summer rain
      on a rose garden.

Such beautiful love we make
  Child's play one moment
               innocent.
Age-old, sophisticated just the next.

Something urgent
    yet everlasting.

Traces of Woman

When morning comes
and you're up before me
    as always
I turn to embrace the pillow
that stills holds your impression

And slowly run my hand
down the sheet
still warm
from your soft woman body.

Just Friends

I hold your hand
as if in friendship
knowing it goes
much deeper
than that.

Feeling that you know it too
and yet
cherishing the pain
of life's strange turns
and holding dear
the things that might have been.

Star Dancer

When I saw her dance
Swan Lake
my heart melted
and tears
welled in my eyes.

Slender muscles
propelled
translucent legs
into leaps
and spins
that belied
the laws of gravity.

To see
such power
from so slight
and beautiful
a form
showed how ignorant I was
about the bounds
of perfectibility
and the generosity
of God.

Middle Age

My mirror tells me
there are places
I can never go again.

If only I'd been warned
that life is a one-way street
I might have watched
my speed.

The Eyes of Youth

Looking deep
>into the eyes of Youth
>I saw reflections
>of Treasures
>I had left there.

Reaching out
>I held the hand of Youth
>and felt again
>the Wonder
>I had known.

Offering my Soul
>I touched the cheek of Youth
>and knew again
>the sweet pain
>of Anticipation.

Impulsively kissing
>the lips of Youth
>I was for a moment
>in a warm place
>I once knew well.

And then

Returning to Reality
        I hugged Youth near
        and laughed
        then cried.
        Then said good-bye.

And in the eyes of Youth
        I saw
        a single
        tender tear.

Why?

They found him
        hanging
in the closet
of his dorm room
at the university.

Such a smart boy
from such a good family.

Everyone wondered
        Why?

Eighteen years old.
Two weeks in college.
Pledging
to the fraternity
of his daddy
    and granddaddy
        and great-granddaddy.

Everyone wondered
        Why?

Being bred
for law school
to join the firm

of his daddy
and granddaddy
and great-granddaddy.

Everyone wondered
Why?

Royalty
in a small town
where he would return
to the big house
of his daddy
and granddaddy
and great-granddaddy.

Everyone wondered
Why?

But he was not
his daddy
or his granddaddy
or his great-granddaddy.

He was sensitive
and tender
and creative.

And he kept asking *Why?*

Why?

Why?

Who Paid the Price

Eternal vigilance is the price of liberty.

— Thomas Jefferson

Freedom ain't easy
and liberty's not free.
A price has been paid
for you and for me.

Soldiers and sailors,
airmen and marines
gave up their lives
to give us our dreams.

In all shapes and sizes,
all colors of skin,
the rich and the poor,
both women and men.

From the north and the south,
the east and the west,
when their country called,
they gave it their best.

In the heat of the jungle,
in the snow and the ice,

in the sands of the desert,
in the seas and the skies.

With their sweat and their tears,
their blood and their lives,
let us never forget
just who paid the price.

The Prison of His Imperfection

Two crippled legs
cast a dark shadow
over his soul.
His deformity
a constant source
of self-indulgent
sorrow.

I never saw him smile
except
at a stumble
by one of the more able
at play
in the school yard.

It was sad how deep
into his self-locked dungeon
his spirit wallowed,
never contemplating
his nearness to the plane
where mere physical infirmity
was of no consequence.

But maybe now
that he has flown
the prison of his imperfection
he can at last indulge
the beauty
that all but he
knew lay within.

Satan and the Preacher Man

And the great dragon was cast out,
that old serpent, called the Devil, and Satan,
which deceiveth the whole world:
he was cast out into the earth,
and his angels were cast out with him.

— REVELATIONS 12:9

He was truly beautiful
to behold
But he had about him
a darkness
that chilled the air.

I've heard
that you've preaching against me,
Mr. Preacher Man,
scaring people with those crazy tales
of a fiery hell
and eternal punishment.

I have, for sure,
Mr. Satan,
been preaching the woes
of eternal damnation
and a hell of fire and brimstone.

Foolish Preacher Man.
There is no fire
or brimstone.
There is only
separation from God
and that is only temporary.

Don't come here speaking lies,
Mr. Satan,
you evil creature.
You cause those souls to betray their God
and be removed from eternal bliss.
You ruin people's lives
both here and hereafter.

Mr. Preacher Man,
I'm not so bad as what you think.
I'm only seeking to
reclaim my rightful place at
the side of God.

But, Mr. Satan.
You have no rightful place
near God.
You are merely a fallen angel
wreaking havoc and grief
for your own selfish sake.

Ah, *Mr. Preacher Man,*
It's merely mathematics.
Now that I have more souls than He
He must admit that
it is I
and not that street magician Jesus
who is worthy to be worshipped.

Mr. Satan,
You're talking foolish.
You're not worthy
to even approach
the Throne of God.

You're wrong,
Mr. Preacher Man.
But then
I don't seek the Throne of God.
I seek my own
for which I'll trade those many souls
who are beyond His reach,
and who become each day
ever more than those who are within.

Why, Mr. Satan,
would God care
how many poor souls
there are imprisoned
in your sorry realm?

Oh, Mr. Preacher Man,
As you have no doubt preached,
He is a jealous God
who mourns each soul
who has chosen to follow my path
instead of His.

But, Mr. Satan,
All you have
are those poor souls
who are not deserving
of His Holy Place.

But, Mr. Preacher Man,
every creature
large or small
is precious in His sight.
And He cannot stand that I have
all those children
who have turned away from Him.

Don't forget, Mr. Satan,
that there will come a time
when He'll reach out
and give them all another chance
to come back into the fold.

Look around you,
foolish Preacher Man.
For every soul He wins,
I win a dozen.
And it will not be long until the day
when He will grant
my rightful place
so that I'll bring him
all these souls that you call lost.

Mr. Satan,
You are clever indeed.
Your deceitful posturing
would almost appear
to have a small ring of truth to it.

And then he laughed
his profane laugh
and turned to leave.
And as he walked away,
the words he spoke
froze my very core:

See you in Heaven, Preacher Man.

OBSERVATIONS

As I grow older
I pay less attention to what men say.
I just watch what they do.

— ANDREW CARNEGIE

Lost Beauty

It wasn't many years before
that she had so much sex appeal
she would raise the temperature of a room
by merely walking through the door.

She was the kind of woman
at whom men would openly stare
and women would watch
out of the corners
of their eyes.

But now Time
is unkindly collecting the fare
  for every late night hour
  and every cigarette
  and drink
  and line of coke.

And she feels
the dark and lonely
   desperation
that only lost beauty can bring.

At the Pink Pussycat

She was almost beautiful
in the blue spotlight
But there was just
a tad too much flesh
on her hips
as she jiggled to
the jungle beat
that filled the club.

And there were a few
little bruises
here and there
Not quite hidden
by the body makeup.

But still
I couldn't help myself.
        She had
        this attitude
        this presence
        that drew me in.

And then
the beat picked up
and the hanging smoke
turned pink

from the light
that caressed
the glitter that lay
upon breasts
too firm
to be sincere
in any other world.

But it was not sincerity
that was on my mind
And I was
even more drawn
to the mood
of the moment.

How could I not be
when every little move
Each subtle wink
made me think
that it was me alone
for whom she moved
so temptingly.

But then I
forced myself
to slowly turn
and look around
at every other
everyman
sitting
in the neon glow
      with bills in hand
      and eyes like puppy dogs
      Who shared my thoughts. . .

And the wonder
of it all
made me marvel.

Hillbilly Heaven

The juke joint smell
    of stale beer
    and cheap cologne
clung to blue smoke
floating like fog
from an old horror movie.

On the band stand
    Six coked-out cowboys
    played *Mustang Sally*
    without listening.

On the dance floor
    Skinny rednecks
    in Garth shirts
    had rock and roll spasm fits
    with chubby country gals
    who strained the seams
    of mock designer jeans.
    Or slow danced
    with double butt locks.

At the bar
      with a half-drunk Jack and ginger
      in front of me
      and a full-drunk honky tonk queen
      beside me
      I grinned and thought:
            I'm in hillbilly heaven.

When The Blues Man
Gets The Blues

*You know the blues ain't nothin
but a good man feelin bad.*
— OLD SAYING AMONG DELTA BLUES MEN

He puts his heart
        into six strings
And bares his soul
every time he sings.
People cheer
when they hear his songs.
But when it's over
and he's all alone
In the dark
        of another cheap motel room
Loneliness creeps in
And morning
can't come too soon.

He hides the dark side of his life
That's filled with pain
        that cuts like a knife
But the cost
        of all the mistakes he's made
Is waiting for him
when he leaves the stage

And fades into the night
with the echo of applause.
          Agony takes hold
          after the curtain falls.

It might be a bottle
          or maybe a pill.
Might be a lady
          selling cheap thrills
Or maybe a white line
          long and deep
Or a little bit of needle
          to help him sleep.

Sometimes I wonder
how it got this way.
He won't talk about it
          But you hear it when he plays.

What remedy can he use
when the blues man gets the blues?

Who'll sing to him
when the blues man gets the blues?

(From a song by Ed George and Danny Angel
on the *Mind Reader* album by Danny Angel and Bo Galigher.)

You Gotta Have a Hat

You know, you cain't play the blues
if you ain't got a hat.
Without a lid on your head,
you cain't be where it's at.

Now, it don't much matter
if it's red or gray,
a British bowler
or a French beret.

It don't make a difference
if it's old or new;
but you gotta have a hat
if you're gonna play the blues.

        Yeah, you gotta have a hat
        if you're gonna play the blues.

You might wear a fedora
like Lonnie J.
or a wide sombrero
like Stevie Ray.

A Panama straw
or a stingy brim
a baseball cap
or a derby like Slim.

It don't make a difference
bout your shirt or shoes;
but you gotta have a hat
if you're gonna play the blues.

      Yeah, you gotta have a hat
      if you're gonna play the blues.

At the Thing Factory

The clickety-click of the Maker Machine
    rings across the concrete
as sparks spark from the welding torch
    and the spray gun hisses paint
    onto the ashy gray of naked steel.

Drills buzz little holes
to be filled by squeaky screws
to form a *Thing*
from a bunch of things.

Hammers smash nails and boards
into crates that will hum down the conveyor belt
to Shipping
with its miles of crinkly brown paper.

The trailer groans and the diesel moans
as the load of fresh-boxed *Things*
    eases from the lot.

Inside
       Accounting scratches up the shipment
       and Sales hears the ring of another call.

Captain Sam

Veterans' Day 1998.
The celebration over
    he was sitting alone
    in the fading light of dusk
    on a folding chair
in the gazebo
on the courthouse lawn.

Around his feeble neck
    on a faded blue ribbon
    the Medal of Honor
from when he'd been an infantry captain
at Normandy.

Gently lifting the Medal
he looked at it as though
it had been a long time
since he'd seen it.

Peering at me
he said
You know, son,
I don't deserve
all this shit.
        I wasn't all that brave.

By the time
I took out
that squad of Krauts
I had been so tired and scared
and filthy and sore
for so long
that it didn't matter
if I lived or died.
            It just didn't matter.

But every year
they drag my old ass
out here
in this wore-out uniform
and tell me
what a big deal
I am.

Then he shook his head
and gingerly stood up
and walked away—
            his withered body
            strained against his cane.

But in his halting steps
there was
a certain dignity
and defiance
never seen
in Captain Sam
            except when
            he put on that tan uniform
            and hung that Medal
            around his neck.

Christmas Cross the Tracks

Christmas dinner
to many
means turkey and ham.

To others
like us
it's kool-aid and spam.

On a table
in the corner
stands a small plastic tree

With red and blue lights
blinking
mockingly mockingly.

Relentlessly
flashing
how barren our station

And how shallow the folly
of our faux
celebration.

Struttin

Hot city streets
    Struttin with a summer beat.
Just got outa Soledad
Everybody know he bad.

His eyes strike fear.
They have the sneer
of a man with nothin to lose.
The taps on his shoes

Keep time to the tune in his head.
A song of dread born in the bed
of a teenage whore
thirty years before

Who spent her nights
in silver tights
on city streets
    Struttin with a summer beat.

Jail

The quality of a nation's civilization can be
accurately measured by the methods it uses
in the enforcement of its criminal laws.

— Justice Louis Brandeis

The smell
of stale grease
and dried sweat.

Desperation
looking to become
panic.

Chaos
disguised by fear
as order.

Bars
binding those
on both sides.

Desert Haiku

Red-orange sky
lights desert sand.
Footsteps drown behind me.

ED GEORGE is a Montgomery, Alabama, attorney and education management consultant who likes to try his hand at song writing and poetry when he's not playing softball or tennis. This book is his second collection of poetry.